The Wisdom of Circles

Gathering Women
for Conscious Community

The Wisdom of Circles

Gathering Women
for Conscious Community

Christine Moses

Cover design by Jenifer Beltz

Back Cover photo by Cynthia Conte

Dedication

This book is dedicated to all the women who have passed through my life, attending my circles, workshops and retreats. Thank you for showing up in the world to do your work, shine your Light, and expand the sacred circles. Blessings to all "mid-life blooming" women, of which I was one. It is never too late to take a different turn at the fork in the road, walk your own path, and manifest your dreams

Contents

Acknowledgements

My deepest gratitude to the following people who have walked with me on my path.

Kathy Grady and Wendy Kopald, the founders of The Women's Circle, I am grateful for your knowledge and wisdom in both the psychology and spiritual fields, and expertise in facilitating, encouraging, and promoting the empowerment of women.

Susan Lipschutz, deep gratitude for opening my eyes to shamanism and how it can help us heal our past wounds, as proof by my first encounter of transformation with you. You are a powerful warrior, wise woman, and I honor you for following your path of the divine feminine.

Barbara Joye, my mentor, dear friend, and wisdom teacher. You were there when I needed you, as were your empowering programs of breath work and leadership. Thank you for your strong belief in me, and for your greater faith of Love and Oneness.

Grandmothers Saundra Pathweaver and Carol Fireheart, for your wisdom and teachings of The Medicine Wheel and Shamanism. As always, when the student is ready, the teachers appear. Thank you for showing me the blessings of signs and synchronicity.

Faith Curtis, my friend, coach and business partner, you are absolutely one of a kind and I love you for that and for your honesty and courage.

Kathleen Rude, lover and protector of Mother Earth, my deepest gratitude for your support and encouragement, and the use of your sacred space for uninterrupted writing.

Kenny Kolter, friend, spiritual partner, skilled drummer — gratitude for teaching me the value and beauty of having a male friend who is filled with honesty, integrity and love.

Gayle Histed, a natural mystic, intentional drummer and reminder of our dreams, and to all the ancestral guides who have passed on their knowledge, teachings and practices, as they crossed my spiritual evolution path.

To the kindest man I know, my husband, Mike. Thank you for loving me and supporting my dreams through thick and thin.
To my three beautiful children, my teachers of unconditional love and the mystery of understanding both simple and profound human needs.

Peggy Kerr, I am so grateful for your unending support, technical knowledge and expertise with hours of editing, formatting and layout, for constantly motivating me and reminding me of the importance of this book, and for your devotion to this project. Without you, this book would not exist.

Preface

Years ago I read Jean Shinoda Bolen's book *The Millionth Circle and* was so inspired by the simplicity of her words *See One, Do One, Teach One*. Her idea of creating community through women's circles motivated me to enter the world of personal transformation. This book is a journey that begins with my own metamorphosis of living a more conscious life and evolves into discovering my gifts, talents and life's purpose in the world.

The structure of the book offers the reader a story of healing, a training guide and empowering inspiration.

Part One **I SEE** is my entry into circles and awakening to a more mindful life.

Part Two **I DO** is my journey that includes powerful insights from experiencing the many circles, and initiation into a deep discovery process.

Part Three **I TEACH** provides experiences simple and practical tools with which to lead circles, concluding with the profound importance of circles in the world today.

I hope my story inspires and motivates you to live a life of joy and connectedness.

The Wisdom of Circles

Prologue

In 1999, I went through somewhat of a breakdown. Some people kindly call it spiritual immersion or spiritual breakthrough, while others laughingly call it spiritual emergency. In any case, I was forty-nine years old, had spent the last seventeen years raising my three children, and was coming to the realization that I was very unhappy. Don't get me wrong, I love my children dearly and had given motherhood my all, happily choosing to only work part time and be a stay-at-home mom. But while I was being a mom and living everyday life, I had never dealt with my own losses and sorrows. The catalyst of my breakdown could have come from the soon to be empty-nesting syndrome, from the possibility of a marriage not completely fulfilled, from the myriad of menopausal symptoms, or from my own deep seeded feelings of inadequacy and invisibility, although back then, I would not have labeled it that way. It seemed like it came to a head quickly. In a moment, I was pulling my car over to a parking lot and sobbing uncontrollably — for what I did not know.

On the advice of a friend, I reluctantly went into therapy, wondering and asking out loud why I was there. I remember saying to my therapist, "I am a woman with three wonderful kids and a good husband, living in a nice house in the suburbs. I should be happy, and really have no right to be here." I knew a lot of women who had seriously dysfunctional childhoods. I felt their problems were so much worse than mine, that, who was I to complain? My therapist said, "don't compare, your story is your story, and your feelings are yours." However, her kind words would take me a few years to understand and accept that—my story is my own, my story matters, and it formed me and my feelings.

So began an intense personal growth path beginning with my journey into many traditions and experiences of self-examination. Never one to just stick a toe in the water with workshops, I dove right into the ocean. There was no preparation for the vast emotional depth I would feel, or the ongoing sense I had of returning to the womb and being paralyzed in my birthing process. I experienced total fear, agonizing discoveries, lost and misplaced feelings, an ever-fragile ego, aching wounds I didn't know I had. And through it all, the verbal self-flagellation... "Couldn't you just leave it alone? Why can't you just be happy? Just let things be." Sometimes, no, quite often, I would want to just go back to the way things were. "The heck with this awakening and spirituality, it was much easier to live with my head in the sand!" But some type of guide or angel or some force would come through with great persistence, and offer some wonderful feedback or synchronistic event to keep me headed on the path, in my case the path of 'most' resistance.

Through my participation in several different types of women's circles, I discovered more than I could possibly imagine in my wildest dreams… a container that has given me a place to be me and speak my truth, a sense of belonging, and an opening to a sacred trust with other women and their stories. These circles have offered experiences on a deep soul level, for discovering the very foundations of whom I am, embracing my gifts and developing my talents. The circles have provided tools and training for my shamanic path and reconnecting with the Earth and Spirit. They have imparted an understanding of humanity, how I can accept both gifts of shadow AND light, and taught me empathy and compassion for others. They have bestowed upon me forgiveness, acceptance and love, for others as well as myself.

At the beginning of my journey, I related to Christiane Northrup when I read her book *The Wisdom of Menopause*. In it she shares "Until then, in my marriage I would continue to play the role of eager-to-please child I had once been, while my husband would fill the role of my remote, emotionally unavailable mother." I too was a sensitive quiet child who would spend many hours alone in a room, listening to music, reading books and fairy tales, and day dreaming at the window. More recently, I found the deeper parallels between Sue Monk Kidd's story and mine in *The Dance of the Dissident Daughter*. She writes, "Now with the wisdom of hindsight, I can look back and understand what I could not really see then – that as a woman I was severed from something deep inside myself, something purely and powerfully feminine…I had no alliance with what might be called the Sacred Feminine. I had lost my connection to feminine soul."

I deeply resonated with her words, of being severed, lost and distanced from the Sacred Feminine. Now with retrospect and a lot of work, I have moved through my healing journey from a personal place of victimhood, which only brought blame, shame and powerlessness, to a transformational place of healing, wisdom, wholeness and embracing the Divine Feminine.

Through the spiritual and practical work of women's circles, we can change the way we think and act, experience our individual transformations and accelerate the growth of consciousness for an enlightened humanity. My experiences offer a real life testament that the feminine nature of the circle yields all this… and more.

Part 1

I See

1 Breakthrough

2 New Awareness

1 Breakthrough

"How strange that the nature of life is change, yet the nature of human beings is to resist change. And how ironic that the difficult times we fear might ruin us are the very ones that can break us open and help us blossom into who we were meant to be."
– from *Broken Open: How Difficult Times Can Help Us Grow,*
 by Elizabeth Lesser

My first entry into a women's circle was what I imagine a baby feels being born–deep and raw emotions of shock and cold, wonder and innocence, an immense storm of change.

The moment my therapist suggested I attend a weekend women's retreat, designed and facilitated by her and her partner, I said yes. I knew I had to be there, even though I knew nothing about it or what would happen. She handed me the brochure that described the weekend. "Women will join together in exploration and growth to strengthen their voice, embrace their courage, honor their compassion, and connect with their heart's wisdom." That sounded lovely. My soul said yes as my more practical head filled with fear.

Big Intentions

As I prepared my mind with packing and arranging schedules with my husband and three children, I also wrote about my emotional intention to do work around my father's death when I was nine years old which had created issues around abandonment and alienation. I naively thought I might put to rest my grief and loneliness in a weekend. My other intentions were to rid myself of negativity, criticalness, self-judgment, and to find my inner strength. I had a big to-do list.

The weekend consisted of many activities all done sitting in a circle on the floor in a large comfy lodge-type room at a campground. I had never sat in a circle with anyone, having worked in the business world with desks, offices, and long conference tables with the leader presiding at the head. I immediately loved the geometry of the circle, its symbolism of equality, and the realization that you could see all others' full faces as they spoke.

Role-playing

The opening campfire on Friday night was engaging, peaceful and intimate as we went around and introduced ourselves. Saturday morning brought new introductions in a deeper way. What followed was shocking. The therapists explained we would do what is called role-playing, a therapeutic technique designed to reduce conflict or revisit relationships with a new perspective. A participant chooses another person in the room to play or assume that character. The first woman stood up, chose her partner, and as we watched the emotions between the two erupt and play out, with great care and guidance from the therapists, you could feel the energy in the room shift dramatically. The horror on the women's faces told all. We were going to spend the entire day doing THIS?

My brain immediately reflected all this back to me, commenting: if you wait and watch this all day, it will become absolutely impossible to get up and do it... I hate being the center of attention and I hate sharing my "stuff" ... This is a nightmare... Before I could even stop it, my body had jumped up out of my back jack to be the second person up on the floor. When the therapist asked with whom I planned to role-play, my now apparently independent-from-my-body mouth said "my mother." Who was this person?

I chose a woman a little older than me with curly white hair, sitting on the opposite side of the room, who looked like she would be a kind mother and very safe. They suggested she stand on a bench so she'd be taller than I. When she stood towering over me, out came years of tears. I proceeded to tell her I was tired of being invisible and not getting the attention I wanted and needed as a child, and much more. The therapists guided us gently to closure. When it was over I felt raw, chilled, as if my guts had been torn open.

The day progressed like that – each person taking their turn to express and claim their feelings and emotions, to state their needs as they never had previously in their lives. One woman left at noon. I wondered if she couldn't take the emotional outpours, or maybe she couldn't be that open, or maybe her wounds were too deep to heal. It takes an amazing amount of courage to be vulnerable, to lay yourself open in front of a group to see all parts of you – fear, insecurities, and even the hidden dark fragments.

Finding Light in Shadows

On Saturday night, we did "shadow" work. The shadow contains all those aspects of ourselves that we hide or deny. In her book *The Dark Side of the Light Chasers*, Debbie Ford writes, "You must go into the dark to bring forth your light. When we suppress any feeling or impulse, we are also suppressing its polar opposite. If we deny our ugliness, we lessen our beauty. If we deny our fear, we minimize our courage. If we deny our greed, we also reduce our generosity... It's about making peace with all these sometimes contradictory aspects of your Self." I had heard the expression "what you resist, persists" but was perplexed by it.

We had to make capes out of black material that demonstrated our shadow parts by sewing and gluing various embellishments. We broke into small groups and each shared what our shadow cape would symbolize. Over the years, I had become an addicted shopper, spending a substantial portion of my part-time employment income on all sorts of material possessions, shoes, clothes, accessories and household décor. My credit card was always maxed and never fully paid off, unbeknownst to my husband or anyone else, and something for which I was very ashamed. So I just decorated the heck out of my shadow cape, sewing and gluing on every embellishment I could find in the boxes to represent all I had needed to purchase and adorn myself with. It was then, after the day's work and creating the cape, I realized my heart had a deep empty hole, and all the obsessive shopping in the world would never have plugged it. As long as I attached my happiness to things in the outer world, this emptiness would never change.

Later that night, we had a beautiful drumming and fire ceremony. We offered up stories about other women who had similar struggles as we did, without sharing their name, but demonstrating our commonalities. We honored the work we had done that day, celebrating ourselves and all women.

Sunday morning brought the "parade of capes." We each stood up wearing our capes and strutted around the room like proud roosters. It was a display of accepting all parts of ourselves, forgiving them, not judging them. This new concept was difficult for me to comprehend. Later in my journey, I would enter another circle and spend an entire year on shadow work, understanding and integrating those parts of myself.

After our closing, we packed and said our goodbyes. With not even 48 hours spent together, so much had been accomplished and experienced; so many lessons had been rendered and many tears had been spilled.

The Drive Home

On the drive home, I broke down crying again and pulled over to park on a side street. Several minutes into my anguish, there was a sudden knock on the window jarring me out of my depths. I looked up to see a policeman staring at me. I rolled down my window and he very kindly asked "Are you OK?" I was embarrassed and stuttered "Oh yeah, I'm fine, I'll be leaving in a second." He replied, "Ok, be careful now." As he drove away, an odd feeling came over me, what I can only describe now as a gentle wash of energy. I drove around back roads for a while, not wanting to go home and face my husband and children with my rawness. I had a severe headache and had never cried so much in my life.

The next week I saw my therapist to process the weekend with her. I was of course complaining to her how I had to face my "mother" situation on the retreat and was disappointed that my "father work" did not appear like I felt it would. After I described the scene with the policeman, she suggested that the policeman was sent to me as a gift to represent my father who wanted to let me know "I'm here with you and was checking to be sure you're OK." When she said this, chills went down my spine as I remembered the shower of energy I felt. While it was a difficult idea to comprehend, it felt "right" in my knowing. I had not had many experiences of synchronicities or messages from the spirit world at this point, at least not that I was aware of. But I knew in my heart that she was right and that he had been there the whole time. And my sister Carol who had died twenty-five years earlier was there as well. A woman in the room chose me to be her mother and role-play issues of her mother work. The woman's name was Caroline, and when I hugged her at the end of our imaginary session, I immediately thought of my sister. These perfectly timed synchronicities came as healing gifts exactly when I needed them.

The grief and crying stayed with me intermittently for several weeks. I had heard that the after-retreat and re-entry back into everyday life sometimes invites more feelings than the actual experience. There were not only my own emotions to deal with, but also the still vivid memory of all those women standing in their own individual truths. I heard so many stories similar to my own—other difficult isolating experiences of alcoholism, ugly divorces, lack of love, abuse, loneliness, fear. They brought me to my first big realization—once we open up, we are all the same.

Hearing all the similar stories awakened in me another fear I had never felt. These women could be my own children one day, talking about me, processing what kind of mother I was for them and dissecting our issues. That was a wakeup call I needed, to understand that doing this work would make me a better person and a better mother. As exhausting and overwhelming as it was, I was completely happy I had attended and done the work. I knew I was headed on a new path in the right direction.

2 A New Awareness

"Things falling apart is a kind of testing and also a kind of healing. We think that the point is to pass the test or overcome the problem, but the truth is that things don't really get solved. They come together and they fall apart. Then they come together and they fall apart again. It's just like that. The healing comes from letting there be room for all of this to happen: room for grief, for relief, for misery, for joy."
– from *When Things Fall Apart,* by Pema Chodron

At the time I did not fully realize I had only completed the first step on my path. One of the purposes of the retreat weekend was to continue with those same women from retreat, forming a circle for sharing and processing. We met every other week for six months and then monthly for about a year and a half. This is where the real work of circle begins.

The Real Work Begins

After the weekend retreat, those women who wanted to continue as a circle met at the therapists' office. There were twelve of us who processed the weekend together. We took turns sharing how it was to return home after the weekend and what came up for us since the retreat. It was good to see everyone again. It felt especially good to me because it was my therapist's office where I felt safe. Two women who were volunteer group facilitators and had attended our retreat were assigned to our circle for the next six months to provide leadership and cohesiveness. They were not therapists but had been chosen by the therapists through an application process to volunteer as leaders who could facilitate our group and keep us on track. We were given the guidelines for circle work and then sent off to schedule our meetings and to decide who would host each one.

Our Simple Guidelines

Our guidelines seemed fairly simple and they had been established and practiced on the weekend.

≈ One person speaks at a time and everyone else listens. No interrupting.

≈ The person speaking should stick to her own story about herself and how she feels about it and not include other people in her life or their stories.

≈ No advice is to be given to the person who has shared; we're not here to fix it.

≈ Feedback can be given, but only from the place of "I", meaning you can say "I know how you feel," showing empathy, not "you should or you can do this" …

≈ Refrain from saying "I know how you feel because my father…" Telling your story takes away from their story and usurps their turn.

≈ It was suggested that the person speaking use a talking stick or stone to demonstrate they have the floor, much like indigenous cultures have used for many years.

≈ If you don't want feedback from another person at the conclusion of your story, say so.

The Circle Takes Shape

While the six meetings went well enough with co-leaders, things got difficult once they left. Personalities began to shape the circle; alphas, as in the animal kingdom, became quickly apparent. Those who were comfortable speaking always went first. Those who weren't would go last and inevitably we'd run out of time, so some might just say, that's ok, nothing's going on with me, or I'm good. We began to use a timer so that everyone would have equal time to share. Also inevitably, someone would be in the middle of their story and ask for just a few more minutes, which created tension with some for not "honoring" the time.

The feedback rule proved especially difficult. There was a narrow area of consensus that often became controversial and created issues of interpretation and application. How do you offer someone empathy but not take over their story or worse yet, sound condescending? Was it really necessary to have feedback? Many decided to forego the whole idea; they'd say "when my story is over, it's over, thank you." Then someone else would WANT feedback because they really wanted advice but we weren't supposed to give it. Or, someone would offer the "bad" feedback by telling their own story of a similar nature, and we would sit there and listen. Then afterward, the person with the most guts would rebuke that person for doing it the wrong way.

Now and then, someone would say something back to someone that was totally inappropriate. Then there would be anger. Or worse—if you couldn't show anger, you might just sit there on a slow simmer. There was always someone who was more sociable and just wanted to chat through the night, a great way to avoid dealing with your issues. Several women dropped out after the first six months. By the end of the first year, we had between six and eight participants at each meeting. Then another problem… If you didn't show up for a meeting and someone had shared something particularly poignant or meaningful, such as a painful childhood event, it felt bad when they came back the next month and others didn't know their story. We had a rule of not repeating a story, so if you weren't there, you missed it.

Staying

I didn't blame others for leaving the circle; it was very difficult to stay at times. "Staying" is what Pema Chodron teaches in her book *When Things Fall Apart*. I didn't read her book until several years later, but was glad to see that I practiced "staying" even when it was painful, when things were falling apart and I didn't know what I was doing there.

Why was I still there?

I was one of the women who would go towards the end or

not talk at all and then feel resentful when I returned home. When I did share, I felt rebuked for telling my story but not sharing my feelings. But I had bottled up my feelings for so long that I didn't know what those feelings "felt" like. I was someone who would not want to give feedback for fear of saying the wrong thing and looking foolish. I was someone who really didn't like sharing her story at all. That's why it was such a shock to me when I jumped up off the floor to be second at the retreat. Why would anyone want to listen to my story?

I told my therapist that my biggest fear was I didn't belong in a self-help group because my problems weren't big enough. I wasn't a recovering addict; I wasn't abused as a child… I went on and on. I had a pretty normal mom with just one problem – she was a functional alcoholic—but she worked hard to put food on the table. I experienced a lot of loss in my childhood, my father and my sister had both died young. But lots of people suffered losses. Did that give me the right to complain and be in therapy? I was afraid everyone was judging me on how insignificant my problems were when compared to theirs.

But, I did need to be there… When someone accused me of not looking them in the eyes when I shared my story, I thought, are you kidding me? I'd never looked anyone in the eyes in my life and it was still difficult a year later in circle. Growing up, I was invisible and I hid in my bedroom—a lot. I could never speak up for myself, I didn't know how to share a story or how to process any problems and I absolutely hated conflict. I always wanted everyone to like me so I became the "good child". Yet, I didn't even like myself.

The Best Thing

If my first year in a circle sounds just awful, it wasn't. It was the best thing I ever did in my life. Where else could you safely experience conflict when you've always run from it? In what other place would you learn to share a personal, intimate story and then listen to someone else's story? How else could you practice using your voice if you have never spoken up for yourself? Where else would you learn not to interrupt or talk over someone, a common occurrence in my childhood?

It was in this "family" of women, whether we liked each other or not, that we could practice how to be vulnerable, to listen and be heard, to use our voice, to trust, to not fix or give advice as women love to do, to forgive, to let go, and to try really hard to be non-judgmental. Our ages, careers, backgrounds and family situations were all different but what we shared was the fact that we were all looking for direction in going through the next stage of life. In *The Way of Transition,* by William Bridges, he states that "Transition is the process of letting go of the way things used to be and then taking hold of the way they subsequently become." We were all living in that in-between stage, trying to let go but not quite ready to become. We shared the same stage in life – the place of healing our wounds and conflicts and struggling to grow into full womanhood.

Circles like this teach us how to "be" in the world. As

difficult as it can be, these lessons and skills can be carried over into all our relationship with spouses, parents, children, friends, co-workers and even bosses. We can be real and authentic but still kind and respectful. We can learn how to clear up misunderstandings without the 'fight or flight' reactions and squelch heated interactions with real dialogue. We can share one another's values and beliefs without judging. We can feel connected in community and commonalities rather than isolated and alone with our thoughts and problems. We can be courageous enough to look at ourselves through the eyes of others. We can be vulnerable and still loved.

Lessons I learned from circle...

≈ The profound importance of listening without judgments
≈ All stories matter, and that nobody's is less or more important than yours
≈ Being open and vulnerable is the scariest thing to do
≈ To look at someone on the other side of the room and feel empathy, even when they annoy you
≈ The acceptance of others just as they are, which meant I had to begin accepting myself just as I was.

Part 2

I Do

3 Next Step: Becoming a Helper

"How might your life have been different if there had been a place for you? A place for you to go... a place of women, to help you learn the ways of woman... a place where you were nurtured from an ancient flow sustaining you and steadying you as you sought to become yourself. A place of women to help you find and trust the ancient flow already there within yourself... waiting to be released... How might your life be different?" – from *Circle of Stones,* by Judith Duerk

One year after I experienced my first retreat, I decided to apply to be a helper at future retreats. You were required to submit a letter describing why you would be a good candidate. In addition to being a participant in your own ongoing circle, you had to be willing to commit to another weekend retreat of new participants, along with occasional training meetings. Additional meetings would be required if you were chosen to go on as a group or circle facilitator.

In my application, I wrote about how much the circle had helped me. It helped me to move out of my head and into my heart. It bolstered me to find my voice over the past year, something that had been tortuous for me before. To be mindful of people's feelings, less judgmental and more compassionate were all huge lessons for me. It taught me how to live more authentically and provided the beginning of my healing from the past. Finally, I wrote that I selfishly wanted to experience the weekend again in a new and different way, perhaps deeper and more connected to myself than before.

Murky Waters

But I never imagined being a helper would be that different from my own experience as a participant—I was so naïve! All of a sudden you are responsible for doing tasks—setting out food, moving furniture, answering questions, and looking like you know what you're doing. (Since I am a former event-planner, that part came fairly easy.) But I entered the murky waters of being an outsider and watching women's emotions stir up while I was still dealing with my own self-criticism and self-worth; the water turned dark and harsh judgments came quickly. I asked myself "What am I doing here, why would you expose yourself this way again? Who do you think you are? You do not belong in this capacity, you are not ready or worthy for this role." In another moment, the pendulum would swing away from criticism and my inner voice said, "I'm okay, I'm pretty good at this because I've been a caretaker a lot in my life. I'm a good listener and I'm present and mindful. I can be detached and watchful and look through fresh new eyes."

Since the retreats were held semi-annually, I was able to return the next season to help at another retreat, this time committing to the role of a group facilitator. Self-doubts began to emerge immediately. My saving grace was the woman I was partnered with had experience and seemed comfortable and confident. Ironically, she had played the role of my mother at my weekend, so at least I felt comfortable with her. While my self-doubts continued, I could feel myself slowly growing in confidence and finding my voice a tiny step at a time. In co-facilitating the continuing group, I had to practice everything I had experienced and learned, yet from the opposite side. The group dynamics were now not "mine." We were responsible for leading the circle through both calm waters and dark clouds, but we formed the walls that contained the circle. We gave it structure, but we were outside of the circle. Again, there were many discussions around the rules of feedback — what exactly is feedback, how does it play out, and the challenge of whether to give it or not. I believed it was better to not offer feedback, to just listen and honor her story — as her story. When I shared, I didn't care about others' opinions or projections. It was difficult enough just to navigate through a new landscape of sharing my story or speaking my truth. But our job as facilitators was not to dictate the way they processed, only to offer the guidelines and explanations and hold the container as tightly as possible.

A Stirring Begins

Watching other women become "broken open" like I had, I began to feel grateful that I could be part of the process. In her book *Call to Connection,* Carole Kammen says this "Call" is "the longing to participate in life in deeply meaningful ways, the inspiration and hope that the very living of our lives would lead us to our greatest potential, the sense of belonging to each other and to the mystery of life." This was the wakeup call to my deepest longing — to be a part of people seeing their potential and participate in "belonging" to this intimate group. The process of circle work was facilitating my personal growth faster than any other way I could imagine. My journal was chock full at this time — of new emotions, new thoughts and awakenings and a-ha moments written at an almost unbearable speed of consciousness. Simultaneously, I was aware of something profound and vital stirring deep inside me, something to come, although I had no idea what that was.

Lessons I Learned from Circle...

≈ We can learn to be open and vulnerable while feeling safe.

≈ We can be honest in our thoughts — speaking them out loud without fear of judgment or blame.

≈ We can find connection with one another and a sense of belonging.

≈ We can find comfort, support, and nurturing.

≈ We can develop our gifts of empathy and compassion.

≈ My healing is your healing. Your healing is mine.

4 Good Medicine

"As children we had spontaneous shamanic experiences, accompanied by a strong sense of oneness with the universe." – Tom Cowan

Through synchronistic events, (there are no accidents!) my next teacher, Susan Lipschutz, was recommended to me for a healing session. While in talk therapy and making progress, I was still struggling with the letting go of past wounds from my childhood and finding forgiveness around my family of origin; I knew I needed some other kind of spiritual guidance.

Deeper Healing

I had two appointments with her, the first to explain what I was dealing with, and the second session was what I now know to be a shamanic healing. I remember vividly, lying on the floor with stones she had chosen to lie on my body, wrapped in a blanket and feeling like an infant. Throughout the session I experienced extreme anger, sadness, frustration, screaming, and then—numbness. Afterward, I felt a deep release both from my body and my heart, and a somewhat peaceful feeling mixed in with more sadness. I was just starting to read and learn about the chakras and how your energy and beliefs are affected by people and situations. I had spent the nineties reading and absorbing many books on spiritual awakening, metaphysics and Native American beliefs and practices and had even taken classes from a Lakota elder. Now I was **experiencing** all this firsthand but really had no idea of what had just happened. I understood though that something profound and meaningful had taken place in my body and psyche.

These sessions became my entryway into the shamanic path. Joining a new circle later that year, led by Susan, I found that my "small inner surge of something more to come" had found me. I discovered a teacher who combined traditional therapy (a trained psychotherapist) with cross cultural spiritual teachings where we were asked to stretch ourselves to possibly — no, definitely — move outside of our comfort zones, inviting Spirit into our lives in a new way. Even though I grew up in the Catholic Church, had attended mass hundreds of times, and appreciated it as a beautiful ritual, I had never embraced Spirit or God in a personal way.

The Medicine Circle

Eighteen women joined The Medicine Circle, a women's group incorporating traditional psychological theories with a particular spiritual growth approach of indigenous beliefs and practices. We met monthly in Chicago, which was a secondary gift to me. Since moving to the suburbs many years ago, I had not taken the opportunity for visits to Chicago, the city in which I grew up and loved. I welcomed the opportunity to be in that energy, meet new women with different viewpoints and, on occasion, visit local stores and coffee shops that were not defined by strip malls.

Tending Our Mesa

I had never developed any spiritual "practices" up to this point. I had no daily or even weekly ritual I could call mine. I knew that my brain and body needed it and that it was time. We began our circle by creating our own mesa in addition to a group mesa, which would provide our foundation of learning.

A mesa is sort of a portable altar or table with an arrangement of ceremonial power objects used as tools for focusing on spiritual forces. Structured to embody the five elements and corresponding directions from this particular Peruvian archetypal form, the mesa becomes a healing place of power. Lovingly created with natural objects from the Earth, such as stones, crystals, and feathers, it provides a way to embody ritual, practice meditation and prayer, and connect with the Earth and our cosmology. As you personalize it and work with intention, the mesa takes on dynamic energies, awakening you to self-awareness and offering itself as a transformative presence.

Being able to transport this portable altar to our circle, and back home to a quiet space provided a path of many new discoveries and understandings of living in a sacred way.

We co-created the group mesa by adding our own stones and objects that were personally meaningful on our journey, as well as one that we thought would be helpful for the group process. At the end of each circle, someone would choose to take the group mesa home and take care of it. This was especially touching if you were going through some trauma or just needed uplifting because it gave you a sense of connectedness to your group during the month.

New Wisdom with the Divine Feminine

In addition to the mesa work, we were introduced to the ways of South American wisdom teachings, from both the Peruvian Andean tradition and the Mapuche, a matrilineal Chilean tribe. These teachings and practices awaken us to our Divine Feminine and show us the deep connections that the indigenous people had with the Earth. By honoring all of the sacred arts — ritual, movement, music, ceremony, prayer, Earth-honoring traditions, creative self-expression, talking circles, journeying, shamanic practices — these ancient teachings can be integrated into our daily lives, bringing harmony and balance. By inhabiting these practices, individually and in community, we can heal ourselves and grow closer to Spirit and to one another.

The "guidelines" of this new circle were very different from what I had experienced. There was no feedback, simply sharing your story, with a quiet moment that followed to honor that story and then moving on to the next. Since I was still participating in my original circle (which lasted two years), I became more aware of the dichotomy between the two energies. The struggles that occurred in my first group from trying to practice the correct way to offer feedback did not take place in the Medicine Circle. While we do see ourselves in others across the room in any circle, mirroring our good attributes and flaws, this circle felt more gentle and safe. Just by being in circle together and witnessing each other's healing process, we were beacons for one another's transformation. We were a circle of women who had more commonalities because we had all chosen *this* particular path for personal growth.

Reconnecting with the Earth

I had to surrender my preconceived notions of my own religion and the cultural beliefs and ideologies with which I was raised. I was forced to look at and let go of judgments that blocked this new found spirituality practice. My naturally skeptical mind and left-brain thinking constantly analyzed, taking literally what everything meant, not understanding the metaphors and symbolism of all these sacred arts and tools. I had a lot of questions, which Susan later joked with me about. But what I knew for sure was that as a child, I loved being in nature. I would sit in an apple tree in the park in front of my parents' apartment and be there for what seemed like hours watching the birds in the trees and the ducks in the pond below. I fondly recalled the innocent and safe feelings I felt and the absolute stillness that being in nature brought me. My connection to nature was reawakening and my love for the Earth was becoming deep and strong.

This work of "reconnecting to the Earth" would quickly transport me out of my left-brain thinking and into my body and heart space. Through many ceremonies and rituals passed on to us by the indigenous leaders and spiritual teachers of the present and past, I would learn the importance of *experiencing*, rather than just reading or thinking about it. This is why the shamanic teachers and the indigenous elders say that the fastest way to transformation is through the path of direct experience. Susan taught and led us through many different kinds of journeys, guided meditations, ceremonies and rituals. She was, and is, an excellent facilitator and beautiful ceremonialist, crafting the integration of these ancient practices into our everyday lives.

Sacred Ceremonies and Rituals

One of my favorite experiences with this new group was an annual weekend spent at a retreat place in rural nature. Fire ceremonies, healing ceremonies, storytelling, journaling, dancing and song… all offered and co-created for transformation, empowerment and a reminder of our roots. With all five of her circles, fifty women, coming together to experience The Goddess Gathering, it was as if we had stepped into another time and we were all part of some ancient tribe of women sharing and celebrating a mystical life together. We embodied the Divine Feminine, sharing purpose and pure love. Joseph Campbell states, "The first function of mythology (myths and mystical rituals, sacred songs, and ceremonial dances) is to awaken and support (in the individual) a sense of awe before the mystery of being." This became my opening into sacred rituals and practices that have been used in all societies for thousands of years. Through these experiences, I learned the importance of doing inner work by connecting to my soul, to the natural world and to Spirit. It opened my heart and allowed my transformational process to flow easier than any other modality.

Creating ceremonies and practicing rituals, just like meditation, becomes habit and has now been proven that these experiences can change your brain patterns into new ways of thinking. It also opens up your creative side and over time you realize that you can create your own ceremonies for any reason and invite friends to be part of that process. Most religions have "rites of passage" ceremonies such as communion, confirmation and bar mitzvah. Our society commonly celebrates birthdays, anniversaries and other milestones. But the practice of embracing all passages including becoming a crone or even death should be embraced, even necessary to honor each person's milestone and to gather us in community coming together to be witness to that person. There is nothing more potent or powerful in a person's life than to have that space honored!

In his book *Creation Spirituality*, Matthew Fox, stresses the importance of the healing arts—ritual, art as meditation, community organizing and community celebrations. "Creation spirituality is all about the healing arts, and therefore, it is about putting people to good work again. Only a finite number of cars can or ought to be manufactured in this world, but when it comes to creativity—to healing and celebrating, to beauty and self-expression—the human species has an *infinite* number of possibilities."

Time to Leave the Circle

Our circle lasted six years, through 2006. During the last few years of this circle I had found another teacher, one who taught more of the North American native ways. I began my studies in the nineties with those indigenous traditions and I was being called back. Toward the end I was beginning to feel more aligned to the new teachings and less connected to the mesa and its ways. I felt called to deepen my studies, to leave the circle and make way for the new. My announcement to leave the circle created quite a stir, with some women agreeing it was time and some overwhelmed at the possibility of not having this connection to rely on every month. I certainly did not intend to be the one who would cause our circle to end, but learned that this is another lesson of being in circle... eventually everything must come to an end. With a great deal of sadness and yet celebrating all we had become, we did close our circle with a bittersweet ceremony. We each wrote something about every woman in the circle, what we loved about each one, and what each woman had taught us. We took turns going around the circle and reading them, a beautifully fitting way to honor each woman and send each one on her next journey.

Lessons I Learned from Circle...

≈ The importance of just listening and honoring

≈ Challenges to think outside the box and let go of old belief systems

≈ The awakening of my intuitive abilities, leading me to deep connections I now have with the Earth

≈ My integration of the Divine Feminine — with singing, drumming, dancing, chanting

≈ Finding my voice

≈ Crying, and even profound sadness, is a good thing

≈ So many synchronicities and a-ha moments, proof of the mystical ways of the universe and creating "awe" in my life

≈ Initiation into my deep healing process

The Wisdom of Circles

5 Student in Training

"You have noticed that everything an Indian does is in a circle, and that is because the Power of the World always works in circles, and everything tries to be round... The sky is round and I have heard that the earth is round like a ball, and so are all the stars. The wind, in its greatest power, whirls. Birds make their nest in circles, for theirs is the same religion as ours. The sun comes forth and goes down again in a circle. The moon does the same, and both are round. Even the seasons form a great circle in their changing, and always come back again to where they were. The life of a man is a circle from childhood to childhood, and so it is in everything where power moves."

– Black Elk, Oglala Sioux Holy man

They say when the student is ready, the teacher will appear. I have always found this to be absolute Truth. Another amazingly synchronistic event happened — the teachers were two sisters, living on opposite sides of the United States, both Cherokee, both Medicine Women and teachers; the students: me, a sister-in-law and brother-in-law from Tennessee, all searching for spiritual guidance and sharing interests in indigenous cultures. Through Spirit, we connected...and together we began our new circle.

Gathering in a New Circle

We gathered our circle of two teachers, Grandmother Saundra Pathweaver and Grandmother Carol Fireheart, and seven souls (one man, the only time I have experienced a circle with a male!) who were willing and ready to dive into a three-year apprenticeship program called *The Medicine Wheel*. Our training would focus on the foundational teachings of the wheel envisioned by Sun Bear, a sacred male teacher of Ojibwa descent and founder of the Bear Tribe in the 1970s. The Medicine Wheel is a circle that encompasses our entire world-the power of the directions, seasons of nature, moon cycles, animals, plants, and minerals. It demonstrates the interconnectedness with humans by teaching us through symbolism about our strengths, weaknesses, challenges and lessons.

Our apprenticeship was so much more than I had even imagined. In the first year alone, besides the teachings of the Medicine Wheel and how to use it as a transformational tool, we learned about the power of intentions and energy medicine. We learned how to move or transform energy, how to read auras, the meaning of colors, the use of crystals, essential oils, how to smudge and the corresponding directional herbs, medicinal plants, animals and their symbolic lessons, the role of karma in the universe and past lives. It was an astonishing amount of information and knowledge to absorb and remember.

Vision Quest

I made the scary but exciting choice of going on a Vision Quest, a native practice of being in isolation for anywhere from 3-5 days, usually outdoors, to contemplate with the spirits of nature animals and plants, uninterrupted. The planned and suggested time was to be out for three days.

For me, the process began a month earlier because Pathweaver explained if I used sugar or caffeine on a regular basis and then had none, I would have withdrawals and only experience one big headache. I weaned off both cravings gradually and by the time I got to the woods just outside of Baltimore, land that was owned by the leaders' friends, I had quit both at least temporarily. The stricter rules of questing sometimes found in other native cultures, like no water or shelter, thankfully were not adopted by my group. As a "city girl", this was plenty of hardship for me—a tent, a hard ground, no food, and nothing to do. Being a nature lover though, I was really looking forward to this and feeling quite brave.

Why Did You Come Here?

When we arrived, we spent the first day in preparation. It included making prayer ties (little cotton squares filled with sacred tobacco and your intentions), having the elders speak to us as a group about the vision quest, and eating very little. Then two questers were paired up to answer two questions: Why did you come here? What are you afraid of? We were asked each question ten times and you spontaneously answered as your partner wrote them down in your journal for you. My answers, I imagine, were common to other folks — to connect with nature in a more intimate way, to connect to the spirit world, to believe that the words I heard from spirit or guides were real, to receive a healing, to sit still, to be open to everything. What I did NOT say was "to receive a vision." I found it comical later when I realized I had not mentioned that as a reason for being there.

What Are You Afraid of?

My ten answers to fears were — insects, having nothing to do for three days, not being able to put my tent up by myself (even though I practiced at home), not being in control of my surroundings, snakes, bored, not being able to hear any messages, insects (repeated) tics (oh that's right, those are insects), boredom, yes, repeated. By the time we got to this exercise, I was in full blown panic. I am very afraid of bugs, not really when I'm gardening, but sleeping in a tent? And I am a high-strung over-achieving multi-tasker. What was I thinking?? I cannot sit for three days and do **nothing**. We were allowed to bring a journal and a pen, and personals. I brought lots of baby wipes to replace having no shower for three days and a small pouch of some stones and crystals I had been working with. I was already very hungry.

The Quest Begins

My quest began well enough. I loved the spot that Pathweaver chose for me, a fairly large space (you couldn't leave your space except just outside of it for your "bathroom") where I didn't feel confined, right beside a beautiful little bubbling stream with fine moss and little plants growing on the river bank. Not having been a camper, I was feeling very proud of myself for putting my tent up efficiently. Among the tree branches, I hung my prayer ties made by me and my feather ties made by the elders as prayers for our vision, then created a little altar with my crystals and its cloth on the edge of the silky moss. I had moved slowly to create my sacred space in a mindful fashion with little effort. I sat down to enjoy my private spot and its beautiful scenery, observing everything around me and writing about it in my journal.

But the first night turned into one big nightmare. I had uncomfortable weird dreams and when I woke up I heard strange sounds all around me that I wasn't sure were imagined or real. I was exhausted but couldn't sleep on the hard ground, hungry with no food…nervous and fearful of everything I mentioned on my list. I realized my tent was on a slight angle, and because of that my sleeping bag kept sliding down and I got up to pull it back up several times during the night. As I tossed and turned feeling the hard ground under my too-thin sleeping bag, I prayed to Great Spirit for something to happen, for a vision, a message, anything. Once in a while in the darkness, I would get just a taste of something spirit-like, hearing horses neighing, the sound of a woodpecker, morning dove, owl, and church music of all things.

The next morning, I woke up so hungry I thought I would faint. Nauseous, weak, and exhausted, I repeatedly wondered how I could sit there for three days. I tried to spend some time writing in my journal, and mostly just stared into the stream or into space. I wrote in my journal that "This is why you don't eat, this is how you become altered; I am so dazed, I'm ready to surrender to anything." Spending the day napping, dreaming (I was having lots of vivid dreams here offering lots to ponder and write about), writing, praying, meditating, staring, napping, I kept hoping for something to happen. Weak and almost comatose by the end of the day, I could barely walk or write. But in my stupor, I was starting to notice, observe, examine every minute detail around me, hearing even the smallest bird or other nature sound, using every cell of my body and mind, and feeling strikingly aware of how insignificant I was.

Facing the Storm

That night, there was a fierce and wild thunderstorm with heavy downpours that lasted it seemed three hours. I would guess from midnight to three a.m. I lay there crying, balling, from every fear you could possibly think of. I heard "things" scurrying around outside my tent, in the pouring rain? My tent will slide away, collapsing, leaving me and my stuff soaked. And then one of the many trees around my tent will fall on me and crush me. Then like the prayers we said as a kid (if you do this for me, please God, I will go to church every Sunday) I prayed that if the tree fell on me, if I was saved, I would do anything he asked. Then I decided to pray that if the tree did fall on me, at least let it take me right away with no suffering. I prayed to every angel, guide and spirit helper over and over to keep me safe. The fear of the storm and all that could happen to me became the impetus for all my life-long, pent-up, never-expressed emotions. Unbridled and unmanageable tears took over my body. I cried for everything in my life, I mean *everything*, and everyone. The storm finally passed just before dawn, which I knew because I woke up to just the first blush of light through my tent, and heard the birds chirping and warbling wildly. It was still drizzling and I thought, wow they don't care that it poured, that there was a thunderstorm and lightning for hours. No matter what, nature always does what it is supposed to do. It doesn't question.

The following morning, I was overjoyed to be alive. Determined to last the full three days, I stayed to late afternoon of the final day and as my reward, I received a wonderful and divine message from my newly discovered spirit guide. Returning from the woods with my gear, filthy, sweaty, exhausted, no longer hungry, I felt happy. I had made the deep connection to spirit. I had received a tremendous and powerful healing through my sorrows. I had found strength and determination. I had the realization, into the depths of my being, that the indigenous belief "We Are All Related" is Truth. And so, it was told to me that I could learn some of the same truths sitting in a circle of nature as I could with sitting in my human circles.

The "Journey" Continues

Our second year of training brought a deeper level of experiences, building on the practices we had learned. We also were taught shamanic journeying (connecting to the spirit realms through drumming or rattling,) the importance of using our intuition through journeying, awakening and refining our psychic awareness, and believing in the messages we received. We bridged a sacred path of the natural world, learning more about our connections to nature—earth, stones, trees—and holding a responsibility to the Earth, and being a steward to the land. We made our own rattles, a medicine tool used for journeying, and a medicine pouch to connect to our own spiritual powers.

We were taught all sorts of healing techniques using many different modalities and tools. We were versed in chants and songs as prayers—to connect us to the Earth, our bodies and our breath. We did meditations to bring in our healing symbols and find our own strengths. We learned about the elements, discovering how to work with them, to bring them into our daily life, and to relate them to our own elemental aspects— another lesson and reminder of our deep connections to the "All."

We learned survival skills, something I never thought I would have to worry about. I was raised in a big city, becoming a suburbanite in my twenties, with everything at my fingertips. When I practiced making a fire from the natural elements—dried leaves, pine needles, twigs and a match, I never got the fire lit. I went through a whole box of stick matches and failed fire! I sure hoped I would never be in a position where I had to use these skills.

Honoring the Lineage

Hungering for all this information, I drove to the Nashville, Tennessee area (nine hours each way) for four weekends a year, and several one day workshops. I was committed to this path, "awakened" yet again, but this one felt like I was home. A lot of people say they know they have been native in a past life and I understand how they feel. I always felt this way but would question it, dismissing my feelings with a "that just can't be" attitude. Now after research and looking back at our history, I think "of course, why not?!" There were literally hundreds of tribes living here, hundreds of thousands of "first peoples" right here in America. Why couldn't we be one of them, if not in a past life, then perhaps at some point in our ancestral lineage.

Here is Grandmother Saundra Pathweaver's (Cherokee, 1941–present) lineage of her training: she was taught by Sun Bear of Chippewa descent (1929–1992) who was trained by his uncles. While she was with the Bear Tribe, she was also trained by Wallace Black Elk (1921–2004), a shaman with many grandfathers who trained him (though not his biological grandfather, Black Elk was one of many); and Evelyn Eaton (1902–1983), born in Switzerland and partly Native, related to the Algonquin of New Brunswick, who adopted Native American spiritual practices later in her life. Pathweaver was also taught by Grandmother Twylah Nitch, founder of the Seneca Wolf Clan, (1920-2007). These tribes, cultures and teachings from various lineages became woven together over time. We carry this energy and "re-member" who we are. I am so honored to be connected to these native ways and philosophies, and to have been trained by such amazing teachers.

After Sun Bear's passing, Grandmother Pathweaver formed the Buffalo Trace Society (BTS) in the same premise of the Bear Tribe, to share the knowledge that had been passed from all her teachers. Within the BTS, Grandmother Carol Fireheart Milliken (Cherokee, 1946–present) trained with Grandmother Pathweaver, Grandmother Twylah Nitch and several other teachers. Together, Pathweaver and Fireheart continue to pass the lineage.

Consciousness Expanding

Our third year raised our consciousness to an even higher spiritual level. We experienced more ceremonies and how to focus intentions, moon ceremonies and how to create them and were offered the opportunity to lead them. We learned how to make the sweat lodge or Inipi (a highly spiritual ceremony for cleansing, purifying and prayer) and the roles of the leaders, as well as experiencing the pipe ceremony—both holy and sacred rites in many indigenous cultures.

By now, we would have heady conversations about all these wisdom teachings, what it meant, human consciousness and how we fit, why we are here. We talked about ancestors and ancient teachers, angels and light workers, and how or where we placed them in the universe, and then how we fit in with finding our purpose. We discussed spirit, creator, source, and what that looked like. We had hundreds of questions for our teachers (well maybe I did.) My mind, heart and consciousness were exploding and I needed answers to so many things in the universe! The best part was during our weekend trainings we shared the house with our teachers, so I was able to go to bed and wake up in the morning, and they were still there! We could see them privately for counseling, dream analysis, or intuitive readings. I'm not sure they thought it was a gift, but I certainly did.

I could not soak up the knowledge fast enough, and just as quickly, I was letting go of the woman I was and re-creating a new me. Dawna Markova describes this process in her book *I Will Not Die an Unlived Life*. "The Native peoples tell a story about Spider Woman who emerges in times of powerful transition, pulling apart the threads that formed the old world and spinning stories that will bring new forms into existence. I think of her part as the woman in each of us that care deeply about what really matters, the part that insists we live our values rather than just talk about them." I understood it was a time of deep transition, of bringing into existence my new form. I felt passionate about this medicine, and my heart and soul were spinning new threads.

Lessons I Learned from Circle...

≈ Our beliefs will be challenged

≈ Recognize that things aren't always as they seem

≈ You can receive an answer from Spirit – just ask

≈ There is no time outside of our physical Earth and there are no limits to our imagination

≈ God, Goddess, Great Spirit, whatever you name s/he – is everywhere and in everyone

≈ We are all One – really!

6 Finding Purpose

"When one hungers for light, it is only because one's knowledge of the dark is so deep."

— Terry Tempest Williams

While fulfilling my commitment to the Medicine Wheel Apprenticeship, another opportunity came knocking for personal growth work. At this point, I was talking to Spirit through my journal entries saying, "Why are you bringing me all this? I don't think I can handle one more weekend, one more training session, or one more circle. And I can't afford this! I must be crazy. Maybe this is a trick to show me what I really need or perhaps learn how to say no." I made lists of everything in my journal that I had going on... I was apprenticing in a three-year program with Pathweaver, still participating in my Shamanic group in Chicago, while working part time as co-owner of a local gift shop and doing small event planning. And oh, I was a wife, homemaker and mother to my three teen to middle school age children, choosing purposely to work part time and be at home more for my kids.

Emerging Healer

I was a classic Gemini, jack of all trades and master of none (an old belief that I have let go of now). Trying not to make random choices on joining more things, I continued to question, wonder, even berate myself each step of the way for taking on too much and being over-committed. But the thing is, I could *not* make these decisions carelessly because each step of the way was led by Spirit. I felt that my body and mind were being re-woven by some unknown force; and even while I was questioning or reprimanding myself, the force would just take hold and make the decision for me. My soul was hungry, starving for its healing, for transformation, for consciousness. As a late bloomer, or a "mid-life bloomer" as a friend recently corrected me, I felt I had waited a long time for this and I was impatient. I was making up for a lifetime. And many times over the past few years, either in my own guided meditations or others' spiritual readings, I had been told I was a healer. How long would it be until I would heed the message!

Breathwork: Integrating Body, Mind, and Spirit

In my quest to deepen and integrate the many lessons I had been taught, I discovered yet another teacher, practice and new paradigm that were to have a major impact on my life. I began to participate in periodic one-day Integrative Breathwork retreats created and led by Barbara Joye.

These intense experiential days proved very healing for me. They provided an opening and awakening to the energy of my body, mind and spirit. Each experience was different. Sometimes I would feel like my skin was peeled back, displaying my deepest raw emotions and heartfelt longings. Another day's experience would offer complete serenity and calm, a feeling of lightness and love for the universe. All of them brought intimate revelations of a new spirit growing inside of me and greater knowing of who I am.

Initiation into Leadership

My great admiration and respect for Barbara prompted me to participate in a three-year program, **Leadership as Service**, created by Barbara to explore our soul's calling and to live our unique path to fulfillment.

I was ready for a different kind of commitment, not more training in the sense of learning or training in spiritual modalities, but in getting to the root of who I was, what I wanted for my life path, and focusing on the healing needed to get there. In *The Feminine Face of God*, Sherry Anderson and Patricia Hopkins talk about looking for periods in your life considered to be turning points on the spiritual path: "These might be specific experiences that lead you to look for different meaning, choices or commitments that you've made, or initiations—both formal and informal—that you have gone through." Even though I did not fully understand the depth of the program, I felt compelled by spirit to join — I *knew* it would offer me a turning point. In retrospect, this experience provided me another initiation on my spiritual path and my unfolding.

Into a New Circle

Here I was again sitting in a group of women, a spiritual

community of seven participants. The first year was grounded in universal spiritual principles. With Barbara's incorporating books by Jacqueline Small, the Founder of the Eupsychia Institute, and many other dense spiritual authors, along with her own expertise and wisdom teachings, a unique foundation was established for the seeds of our personal growth search. We were supported in releasing the toxic belief systems and wounds that influenced us long ago, set by family, culture and society. Learning the principles of transpersonal soul-based psychology which incorporates the spiritual aspects of self-development, we began to access our own vital energies and wisdom, awakening our intuition or our Higher Knowing. As Jacqueline Small states in *Psyche's Seeds* "There can be no outer experts on the path of self-knowledge; the learning comes from within."

The second and third years of the program offered a process of total immersion into a deep healing process and the emergence and discovery of my Purpose. We investigated and identified our core values, defined our personality traits through the Keirsey Personality Test, and dove into Stephen Karpman's work of the Drama Triangle to explore the three psychological roles of Persecutor, Rescuer, or Victim.

Into the Shadow Again

We excavated our shadow parts, making masks to symbolize our shadow aspects, one of the deepest processes I've ever experienced. Working with a conscious effort to discover the part of ourselves we hide or don't like is definitely the hardest psychological work one could do. In his book *Spiritual Bypassing*, Robert Masters points out, "Eventually, if we continue going more deeply into the work, our habit of distancing ourselves from shadow elements is replaced by a compassionate, courageous embracing of whatever we have disowned, marginalized or rejected in ourselves… as we free its energies and develop a genuine intimacy with it, we experience true integration… manifesting as a deeply felt sense of wholeness, balance and integrity."

I thought back to the first time I dealt with shadow in making the capes at my initial soul-searching retreat with my therapist. I realized that had only been a beginning. This shadow work could be a nightmare! I wanted to run away at this point, as I'm sure many of us did. Somehow I knew I had to stand in the fire and immerse myself in the healing process. I was holding a lot of anger, resentment, sadness and judgment towards myself and others, wounds that had festered and deepened for a long time and that I had ignored. "To heal is to make whole. And what is whole can have no missing parts that have been left outside," states *A Course in Miracles*. Where else was I going to go? I discovered that even though I was terrified, once I began the inner work journey, I could not go back.

Answering My Soul's Call

In the final year of the program, we drew on all of

our previous work to help us choose and create a personal action plan for our own individual "calling." Because my Gemini spirit and personality carry a natural sense of order and organization and a wearing of many hats, I had a million ideas of what my plan or calling should be, depending on the day and the time.

I went through a supportive and guided process with Barbara reflecting on all my ideas. They ran the gamut... house and closet organizing from a spiritual perspective, getting through times of transition and letting go of these things that no longer serve you and weigh down your life... then helping to create a "church with no walls", offering programs and teachings to all beliefs and all walks of life, and where all spiritual practices would be welcome... life coaching, focusing on helping people though transitions... and several others. All of the ideas included the theme of community and I was confident in my ability to build relationships and trust. I thought I would make a good facilitator or leader in any of these places. To overcome my fear of public speaking, I even joined Toastmasters.

After contemplating all of my ideas, I realized that since my heart had been opened with women's circles, this would be my focus.

I have since facilitated at least fifteen different circles of women with diverse backgrounds containing four to ten participants. I have used different intentions, themes, and time frames. As a backbone for the circle, I have used various books and oracle cards. I have created my own programs with themes such as

"The Heart of a Woman" and "Walking the Sacred Path', in addition to utilizing the energy of the seasonal changes and indigenous medicine teachings. Each theme or intention attracts different women and their interests. But every woman enters the circle because she wants to tell her story (even if sometimes reluctantly) and have someone really listen, wants to have a place where she feels she can belong, a safe place to have a deeper connection with her spirit and soul. Regardless of the focus of the circle, we listen, learn, witness one another's story and honest feelings, cry and laugh with one another. We share in each other's growth and the potential to become healthy and whole.

All of the years of learning, all of the exercises, all of the ceremonies and rituals were finally coalescing into how I would live my Purpose and the three roles through which I would express it: Healer, Leader, Teacher.

Lessons I Learned from Circle...

≈ Commitment… the first step of transformation is to show up.

≈ The more you share your vulnerability, the easier it becomes.

≈ Forgiveness and shadow work is an ongoing life process.

≈ Adaptability and openness to flow is key to the transformational process.

≈ Be open to the surprise!

The Wisdom of Circles

52

Part 3

I Teach

7 Creating a Circle

"Being in a circle is a learning and growing experience that draws upon the wisdom and experience, commitment, and courage of each one in it. As we begin to change our personal relationships, that change spreads. It's like throwing pebbles in a pond; each one has an impact and an effect, with concentric rings of change rippling out and affecting other relationships."

– from *The Millionth Circle,* by Jean Shinoda Bolen

Gradually an idea began to emerge in my head. I had now taken part in four different types of circles and each time I participated, I thought "I could be good at leading this." Of course, as soon as I thought that, the opposite reaction and the reprimanding voice would enter my head. "Who do you think you are? You're not trained, you're not a therapist, you have no background in this, no degree, no, no, and double no." So needless to say it took some time to come around to this. Several years before, I had read Jean Shinoda Bolen's *The Millionth Circle* and had been so inspired by the simplicity of her words *See One, Do One, Teach One.* What a concept – to just see it and do it. If the voice in my head kept saying "I could be good at this," then I had to at least give it a try. I had worked hard to let go of my judgments of not being good enough. By the end of 2005, I had been in circles and in training (along with receiving my master degree in Holistic Ministries) for seven years... transforming, evolving, moving into who I truly was.

Enough was enough – time to free my doubts and bring out the gifts of me!

Throughout the next ten years I created and led many women's circles and retreats. I witnessed transformation in many women's lives. To go beyond Jean Shinoda Bolen's call of "See One, Do One, Teach One," I wanted to guide other women in my circles to go out and facilitate new circles of their own in order to pass on this vital work of the heart, mind and spirit.

The following material includes suggestions and practices that I hope will support many others to create new circles, leading us closer to the "millionth circle."

What is a Women's Circle?

A women's circle is a sacred place where our voice can be heard and where our story matters. We can find comfort, support and nurturing. We can learn to be open and vulnerable while feeling safe. We can be honest without fear of judgment or blame. We can find connection with one another and a sense of belonging.

Through the spiritual and practical work of women's circles, we can do the work of the Heart, change the way we think and act, and become a more authentic Self. We can experience our individual transformations and accelerate the growth of consciousness for an enlightened humanity.

It is the energy of the Divine Feminine. Our western model is the masculine, where the individual does their work alone to heal. Through the energy of the feminine, we heal ourselves, we heal each other, and ultimately we heal the planet.

"My healing is your healing. Your healing is my healing"

Setting Intentions, Themes and Outcomes

Decide on your focus, intention, and purpose for your circle. By creating your intentions in the beginning for the women who attend, the purpose will naturally follow.

Make a list of all possible intentions and how you want to impact their lives. What are their general needs and how will you meet them?

The following is a list of possible intentions, themes and outcomes.

Possible Intentions

- Teaching and understanding of a deep connection or relationship to Spirit or Self
- Provide journal questions to open them to new possibilities; example: what would you do if you had NO barriers...
- Open them to the possibility of using tools and practices
- Honest feedback & feel safe in questions – let us know if they don't "get it"
- Importance of taking time out for yourself
- Offer examples of ritual & ceremony for everyday life
- Experience music & song
- Get out of one's head and into the body & heart
- Time and space for reflection and self-discovery
- To experience a connection with others
- To experience a connection with nature

List your ideas here:

Possible Themes

- General personal and spiritual growth
- Program development (your particular area of expertise or training)
- Wellness: nutrition, exercise, lifestyle
- Intuition and inner-guidance
- Self-esteem building
- Meditation or Mindfulness
- Nature connection, seasonal themes and transitions
- Spiritual book group – using a specific guide, book or spiritual teachings as a learning and integrative opportunity

List your ideas here:

Possible Outcomes

What do you want them to leave with? Again, create a list for yourself.

These are some of mine, you will discover your own.

- A sense of belonging, that you are not alone

- Our experiences are actually universal experiences

- Increased confidence in the ability to express yourself

- Greater appreciation of their own gifts in the world

- An increased sense of self-esteem

- Increased sense of courage

- Leave feeling empowered or motivated

- Speaking honestly and boldly

- Learn and have authority in your life to speak up

- Increased capacity to listen to others, no matter where they are

- Helps to build consensus

- Living mindfully

- Leadership development

- Restoration of spirit

- Leave feeling valued, accepted and affirmed

List your ideas here:

Forming the Circle

Who, what, when, where and how…

Who

It's important to contemplate these questions when determining your audience:

- Who are you trying to reach?

- Who will you invite, perhaps based on your specialty, practice, or focus?

- How many will be comfortable for you?

- Are they a good "fit" for you, for your first time?

What

What is your purpose or intention for the circle, based on your specialty or practice? Writing out your intentions for the circle helps to make your purpose clear in your own mind, as well as sending it out to the universe — and practical marketing.

Where

It's important to utilize a location that is comfortable to you and your participants.

- Do they need to have comfy chairs, or can they use floor pillows or back jacks?

- Is it warm and inviting? Does it FEEL good?

- Will it always be in the same location, or will you move locations?

In paying attention to this, you will also begin to learn about energy, an important element of all circles. (See chapter 8.)

When

- Determine the dates and times, when and how often you'll meet and then commit to these.

- Consider weekly, bi-weekly, monthly.

- What is the duration or length of the circle?

Mine have transformed from a weekly circle, for eight weeks or so, to a monthly circle for six to eight months, and even a year.

Commitment

Clarify the commitment expectations of this circle:

- Is it an open circle or will you require a commitment from the participants?

- If so, for how long? An open circle means anyone can come/drop in, without notice. This is fine if you have a core group that you can rely on.

- Think about the value of your time and energy, as well as how you will develop trust in a drop in circle, where different folks show up at different times.

Fees

Consider the following variables:

- Length of time for each circle

- Your preparation time and

- What value you place on your time and energy

- How often you will meet

- An offer of a discount for advance payment for the whole commitment.

This may be your way of service in the world so you can offer it for free. Perhaps you may request a "love offering" for your service of whatever they are able to give.

8 Facilitating a Circle

Many books include guidelines, principles or contracts for doing personal growth work in circle. Over the years, this is what I have learned and know to be MY truths:

≈ A circle is a place where we are heard and witnessed.

≈ A circle is a place where your story matters.

≈ A circle is a place where we can find comfort, support and nurturing.

≈ A circle is a place to be completely present, in the moment, with no distractions from the outside world.

≈ A circle is a sacred and safe container for who we are and who we can become.

≈ A circle is where all beliefs are welcome.

≈ A circle is where one person speaks at a time; we honor their voice.

≈ A circle is where we practice intentional and conscious listening, without thinking or planning <u>our </u>thoughts.

≈ A circle is where we learn non-judgment. What we <u>all</u> feel and say has value

≈ and no one has walked in another's shoes.

≈ A circle is where we learn to trust – in ourselves and others. Everything that is said in the circle stays in the circle.

≈ A circle is where we can learn to be open and vulnerable.

≈ A circle is a place where all emotions and feelings are welcomed – sadness, loss, tears as much as joy, happiness, and laughter.

≈ A circle is a place where we do not "fix" others or their situation, only listen. Feedback is invited... a choice.

≈ A circle is where we might see ourselves on the other side of the room, and choose to like it... or not.

≈ A circle is a place where we will find challenges – to accept, to discern, to think outside the box.

≈ A circle is a place you can receive a-ha moments because we all learn from each other.

≈ A circle is where you can practice forgiveness.

≈ A circle is where we find God, Spirit, the Divine, because it exists in everyone in the room.

≈ In a circle, we discover that everyone is unique, yet the same.

≈ In a circle, we can find autonomy, empowerment, respect, strength.

≈ In a circle, we can find the meaning of Oneness.

≈ In a circle, a woman can claim her life.

Preparation

In creating a circle for safety, sacredness and sharing, it's important to prepare the space ritually and energetically as well as create openings and closings for the circle.

The positive energetic feeling of a circle is dependent upon the leader holding a container that is safe enough for women to express fully and safely. Using the guidelines and a few of these suggestions will help you establish that safe, loving container for women to attend and one in which they will want to return.

Creating an altar

Chair placement of a circle allows the center space to become the perfect place for a small table or the floor to be an altar or focal point.

You can use:

- a candle that will be lit at the beginning of the circle

- a chime or bell to bring everyone into a quiet space

- sacred herbs such as sage to smudge/clear the space and the participants

- sacred or meaningful objects you may wish to place on a table

- a "talking" stick or stone to be used by each participant taking turns

- A talking stick is a tool used by many indigenous cultures or traditions to discuss a problem, allow all viewpoints, and make decisions. The stick (or some use a stone) is passed from person to person as they speak and only the person holding the stick is allowed to talk during that time period.

This recognizes the value of each speaker, and reminds each person to practice conscious listening and not interrupt.

Centering the Circle

All of the above objects also can be used to "center" everyone after they arrive. After everyone's busy day, it is vital to create an environment that calms people at the beginning of the circle.

Opening Ritual Ideas

In addition to the above altar rituals, these ideas can be used for openings:

- Prayer, Invocation or "calling in" by the facilitator. Many forms are available that are non-secular.

- After a participant says her name, the group repeats the name with a Welcome. Example "Welcome Chris." This is also a great tool with which to remember one another's names.

- Meditation; a brief body/mind check in, again to calm nerves and release mind chatter from the day

- Music/song/chant; any piece that is calming or appropriate to the theme you have chosen

- Readings—from a poem, quote or book (which may lead into the night's theme)

My Simplified Guidelines for Circle Participants

These serve as reminders, for yourself as well as the participants. You might want to create your own.

- One person speaks at a time.

- Each person speaks from the heart and uses "I" statements in their sharing.

- Practice conscious listening.

- We listen with non-judgment.

- We're not here to "fix" one another or their problems, only to listen.

- All emotions are welcome.

- All beliefs are welcome – no one gets to be wrong.

- Everything that is said in the circle is confidential.

- Share to your comfort level.

- You don't have to share, but I encourage you to!

- (If using a talking stick or stone) When a person is holding the talking stick, only that person speaks.

Challenges of a Circle

Regardless of what type of circle you have created, whether a simple meditation group or a circle of personal growth through the various uses described in this book or others, there may be challenges. Whenever you bring a group together of diverse personalities, there could be folks in the room who are a challenge to have in circle.

We each encounter people in life who remind us of our family members or a situation that perhaps has not been psychologically addressed. There may be someone who sees the person across the room as a reminder of someone who has wounded them, or perhaps reminds them of themselves. In psychology, this is called mirroring. We can see a behavior in someone that we don't like about ourselves but have not yet consciously admitted. There are many books written by experts on this if you wish to research more.

When there are any problems of confrontation, boundaries, dominating, advice-giving, judgment, etc., this is your opportunity to remind everyone of the guidelines — again, particularly speaking from "I" statements rather than "he, she or you said or did that" which takes us into blame and shame. The leader is responsible for holding the sacred space with respect and empathy for all. The practice of being attentive, listening to their stories, withholding judgment, and reminding them of the guidelines will support the leader as a role model for others.

If one is unable to follow these guidelines, it may be necessary to ask the person to leave the circle. This may be best for the good of the whole. Always try to have some closure around the person leaving the circle, for the participant as well as the rest of the group. Brushing it aside and NOT talking about it will produce the elephant in the room effect. Talking about it, without judging the person who has left, will offer healing to the group, and may even help one see and understand a similar situation in their life.

Experiences, exercises and tools

Journaling

- I Am a Woman Who…. exercise: Write down this beginning sentence in a journal and finish it as many times as you can. This is a simple yet profound way of self-discovery.

- Questions to invite thinking, open-mindedness, new ideas, or blocks and challenges. They offer insights for themselves and for you and everyone else to know them on a deeper level. See following examples.

- Questions framed to ask "what blocks you from…" or "what keeps you from…" is a powerful way to delve deeper into what it is that stops you from being or living your desired path.

- Journal using the concept of five gratitude's a day; write five things you are grateful for… when you wake up in the morning, or before you go to bed at night. (per *Simple Abundance* by Sarah Breathnach). Especially good for those who are negative or have old or limited beliefs.

- Create a list of intentions which can be turned into goals, or steps, which then can also be used as affirmations or daily reminders.

Sample Questions for Journaling

Take some time for breathing and centering before any exercise in journaling.

These questions are from Professional Certified Coach and Retreat Leader, Karin Marcus http://steppingoutcoaching.com/

- What do I want to invite into my life?

- What do I want to create?

- Who do I want to become?

- What direction in my life is longing to grow?

- Is there a project I've been longing to complete?

- How can I find balance in my life between personal life, family and career?

- How can I nurture and listen to my inner voice of wisdom?

- Is there a habit I am ready to shed?

- How can I have a healthier body?

- How can I have a more compassionate heart?

- Do I need to re-awaken my spiritual being? How can I do that?

You can transform your answers to these questions into intentions and affirmations.

Sample questions used in my circle "Walking the Sacred Path"

Good for women to get an overview of their current lives; leads to awareness, and good discussion among participants.

Write the answers for yourself!

- What changes have had the greatest impact on your life in the last 5 or so years?

- What changes, if any, are you having difficulty or have had difficulty accepting at this stage of your life?

- How have you overcome this difficulty if you have? If you have not, what do you think is holding you back or blocking you?

- What behavior, patterns or approaches do you find are no longer useful or beneficial at this point in your life that you would like to shed?

- What specific changes would you like to make in order to increase your physical, emotional and mental well-being?

- Do you take time for nurturing yourself? This is not only physical, like massages, or mental, like reading, but spiritual-based honoring of yourself, such as taking time for music or art. If so, what do you do towards that end? If not, what would you like to do?

- As adults and elders, we have so much to give. Name at least three talents or gifts you have to offer. (Perhaps you haven't used them yet and even keep them hidden.)

- If there was one thing you could change about your life, what would it be?
- What would you want to create for yourself if you could drop **all** barriers — self-talk, buts, ifs, reasons why it can't happen, etc.

Meditation

There are so many types of meditation and literally hundreds of books written about the how and why. Any style would be good to incorporate during a circle to bring people into a calm relaxing place after their busy work day. These are just a few ideas:

- Traditional eastern meditation where you sit and think "no-thoughts" and focus on the breath

- Guided meditation or guided imagery
- Music for relaxation or visualization (see Resources)
- Walking meditation for being mindfully aware and observing your natural surroundings
- Body scans create awareness of physical blocks (as taught by Jon Kabat Zinn)
- Mindfulness creates awareness and connection to the body in everyday living

Ritual and ceremony

Offering ceremonies or rituals as part of a circle is an experience that can bring you closer to Spirit, to nature, to one another and can nourish our lives in a unique way. The indigenous people have long known that the experiential path is the fastest way to transformation because it involves all parts of you – body, mind and spirit. You can create simple rituals that are inspiring and fun, as well as deeper meaningful ceremonies to help through a life transition.

- Welcome "name" to each in circle

- Create an altar, as part of your own sacred space or for use in the circle space. There are no rules here—whatever symbolic items that speak to you can be used, in addition to nature items and a candle. Beautifully illustrated ideas are in *Altars*, by Denise Linn.

- Seasonal changes and its symbolism that connects us to our natural surroundings. Book recommendation: *The Circle of Life*, by Joyce Rupp & Macrina Wiederkehr.

- "Honoring the directions" from the indigenous ways may speak to you as an opening or a ceremony.

- Full or New Moon; again there are rituals on the internet and many books about these auspicious times.

- Rites of Life passages: honoring life transitions such as divorce, marriage, empty nesting, grief or loss, death.

- Smudging or clearing yourself and your space; can be done with a variety of herbs or even sound such as drum or rattle.

- Using stones or crystals in which to place your intentions at a particular time or life phase and return to the Earth when it feels complete.

- Fire ceremonies to release or let go of that which no longer serves you.

Creative Expression

I use art in my circles to explore and express one's inner feelings, heart and psyche, a visual way of working instead of journaling. It's important for women to let go of that critical voice that says I am not an artist or I can't draw. Learning that art is meditative and images and symbols can bring unconscious beliefs or thoughts to the surface can evoke new awareness of who we are. None of these require an art background or experience. It is purely for your soul's expression and self-discovery, so there is no judgment around talent. There is a plethora of information on the internet about these creative modalities.

Collaging — general form of cutting pictures and words that speak to you; meditative and fun

Soul Cards — a form of collaging, a creative process with particular symbolism that I find addicting

Vision Boards – made for envisioning and manifesting goals and creating empowerment; lots of information on the web about this

Mandala Making – extensive work of Carl Jung; a process of art that is meditative and self-reflective, can unlock secrets and desires

Mask Making – a form of creativity that invites one to explore various aspects of one's personality. I find this to be fun, creative and can be a deep process. Use plastic masks from a craft store rather than the original but difficult form of applying papier mache to the face

Prayer flags – create these together in Tibetan style with prayers/intentions written on them. Beautiful group activity to then take home and display outside

Other Tools

Choose a "reading" or a passage from a book that offers a topic for the circle

Divination cards, used as a focus for the night, then discuss what it means and how it relates to what is happening in your life or situations. Examples: Osho cards, Medicine cards by Jamie Sams (animal symbolism), Angel Oracle cards by Doreen Virtue

Daily devotional books make good topics; see References

Particular teaching areas in which you have training, strengths or talents

Psychological tools you may know

Closing Ritual Ideas

When circles are not properly closed at the end, it feels like people are left hanging, whether it is the end of the evening or the official closing of a completed circle. Remember, you are closing a sacred space both physically and energetically for the group. You can close each circle with any of these ideas.

- Music/song/chant

- Holding hands in the circle for gratitude or particular intention; this can be shared by all

- Prayer led by facilitator for the appropriate theme that night

- Any words from leader, i.e.: until we meet again, the circle is now closed, etc.

- Using a "one word" check out; each person goes around in the circle and says one word of how they feel at the end. (Stress that all words are acceptable, good or bad. These are their feelings.)

- Blow out the candle

Closure for Ending Circles when Complete

- Have each person write a letter, note or poem, to each other woman and share what they liked about her, or what they learned from her.

- Each person brings a small gift for each one (not store bought) such as a stone or other nature object, statue, spiritual object; something that reminds them of each person. Go around one at a time and give the object, explaining the significance.

- Each of the above ideas is a deep honoring of one another and the time spent together.

- Possibly provide a follow up meeting with updates and "check ins" at a later date.

9 Promoting a Circle

Creating a source from which to advertise your women's circle is important. It could be as simple as an E-blast to your friends and potential clients with a friendly "pass it on".

It will help expand your potential audience if you use the internet wisely.

Networking

This is most important! Attending networking events where women are — works! Also, and just as good, scheduling one-on-one coffees or lunches to get to know one another better. This is a personal time where you can connect with someone and really tell them what you do. Showing interest in someone else's work and life invites interest in yours so it becomes a mutual effort, not just you marketing your business.

Website

Create your own or have someone else do it for you. If you don't have one, start out simple.

E-Newsletter

Straight email is fine for less than a list of 50 or so people. Once you've grown to more than 100, I recommend using an online marketing service such as Constant Contact or Mail Chimp. Sending E-blasts with INTERESTING notes, observations, and/or photos is the key. It keeps your customers abreast with what you're doing and interested in following you. Start forming an email address list now, with all friends and family!

Social Media

Facebook, Twitter, Linked in, Instagram, Meetup... There are constantly new sources of social media! Rather than using a hodgepodge of them, I find the best success comes with limiting yourself to one to two sources and fully using them to engage your clients. Deciding which platforms to use will probably depend on the age of your audience.

Strategies for increasing attendance to your circles:

- Offer a discount with advance payment for the series – "early bird fee".

- Offer a discount for bringing a friend.

- Consider partnering with someone; although the fees will be split, this doubles your potential audience.

- Create a flyer, take it with you. Talk it up everywhere you go!

Helpful Hints for Registration

- Ask for the fee, or at least a deposit, in advance. This way, you know they are serious. You may get seven or eight women who say they are coming the first night but only a few may actually show up if they haven't paid. Make them commit!

- Always follow up with each person after receiving their registration to immediately engage them and show your appreciation.

- Be sure to have options for payment, including credit card, through your website or other merchant services.

Your minimum or maximum number of participants is dependent on your energy level. Ideally, you would like five or so for your first one. Remember that on any given night, even with prior commitment, there may be one or two people missing which may change the energy of the circle.

Again, think about how you value your time. When first starting out, you may be willing to offer this circle support complimentary. Take into consideration your time and energy spent on marketing, planning, emailing and the follow up for each circle.

All that being said, KNOW that you are growing this concept and you are out planting seeds and inspiration for women everywhere!

Sample Registration Form   Information

Name:

Address:

City: State Zip

Phone: Please include all in case I need to reach you.

Mobile   Work

      Home

Please write a few sentences about why you were "called" to join this circle/class. This is just to help me know you a little better, if I don't already.

Please return this commitment form with your payment of $_____ covering _____monthly circles.

—OR—

Two payments of $_____: first payment due _____, second payment due_____

If you need to make other payment arrangements, I'll be happy to discuss by phone

Make check payable to …. (or offer a place for credit card information.)

Return to… (Provide your name, address, email, phone number so they can reach you with questions.)

10 Call to Action

"What the world needs now is an infusion of the kind of wisdom women have and the form of the circle itself is an embodiment of that wisdom… This is what equality is like. This is how a culture behaves when it listens and learns from everyone in it."
—from *The Millionth Circle* by Jean Shinoda Bolen

At the beginning of my journey and the discovery of circles, my therapist suggested I read *The Millionth Circle*, by Jean Shinoda Bolen. In it, Jean proposes that when we have a proliferation of women's circles, we will reach a tipping point of bringing humanity into a post-patriarchal era. This holds the promise that when a critical number of people change their attitude, behavior or thinking, culture at large will change and shift and a new era will begin.

Creating the Ripple

Every time I lead a circle, I believe I am contributing to the shift of consciousness of many people, and helping to lead us to that tipping point. Each woman who attends opens her heart to a new way of thinking, changing her perceptions, the way she thinks, acts and behaves toward her family members, friends and her Self. She may discover her own voice, her inner wisdom; feel more creative, conscious, or empowered. Then each of those people that she comes into contact with is changed in some way by observing her new behaviors of perhaps openness, kindness, acceptance or compassion for others.

And it does not matter if the circle's intention is as simple as learning to be mindful (although we all know that is not easy) or as complicated as a group of politicians trying to come to a consensus. We have become a world of people who believe that all of us are separate and disconnected from one another and the natural world. But circles can make a difference in the world, moving us from separation to connection. If we sit and practice the guidelines of the circle, the ripple effect has been put into play. We create a momentum, connecting to one another in a deeper way, and making a difference, first to our family, then to friends, then in the world.

My friend Laura has been in one of my ongoing circles for five years. She describes it as a beautiful process to witness. Each time you are invited to be an active listener to another woman's story and journey, we watch her emerge with an "aha" moment of clarity as her physical and spiritual bodies move closer to the authentic self. Laura also leads women's circles, but always tells people that her own circle is the gift she gives to herself every month.

Ginger, who is new to circles and has also taken my facilitation training, appreciates the sacred atmosphere of support and security. "In circles, I have witnessed great things happen. I am always in awe of the deep transformative energy that a group takes on as each individual allows themselves to sit authentically with the support of others." This theme of authenticity keeps repeating because the circle is such a unique atmosphere where people can share their honest feelings without fear of judgment.

Global Empowerment Through Circles

Throughout the world in the last several decades, there are many examples that the value of sacred circles is being recognized. In her book *My Life on the Road*, Gloria Steinem talks about going to India and listening to the issues of the local women. She comes back again and again to the idea of people sitting in circles, saying "one of the simplest paths to deep change is for the less powerful to speak as much as they listen and for the more powerful to listen as much as they speak." Applying the principles of really listening to their needs and desires and then mutually sharing ideas demonstrates the positive results of what happens when people are given a voice. It's a two-way street since the one that is listening to their needs is educated about their story, culture, or situation, resulting in empathy and compassion.

Today, Jalaja Bonheim facilitates circles between Palestinian and Jewish women, co-creating a space for changing how we perceive ourselves and others. By approaching them in this manner of respect and curiosity, they can move toward empowerment and integrity. I look forward to sacred circles being offered to openly discuss racism, tolerance, separatism, the polarization of our cultures and society and moving toward the consciousness of the whole.

The Acorn Women's Cooperative is a Tanzanian NGO that is another example of a circle and close to my heart. When *It Can Be Done*, a non-profit dedicated to clean water in Uru, Tanzania, began to bring clean and safe water to the people in the Kilimanjaro area, the women saw an opportunity for income producing activities. With less time spent acquiring water, it opened the door to economic empowerment, leading women to new levels of decision making, community participation, social justice and creating changes for a better life. The common goals and intentions established in their group have taught them active listening, sharing ideas and making decisions for the good of the Whole. By sitting and brain storming together, these women have learned the same principles of the circle, resulting in cooperation and collaboration while building their business model.

Circles Are Timeless

The circle is not a groundbreaking framework or a new paradigm. Throughout our history women have gathered together in circles. From groups of women quilting and sewing together to consciousness raising groups of the seventies, we have united in listening, learning, comforting, supporting, nurturing and loving one another. By sharing individual talents, collective wisdom and collaborative thinking, we have rallied and triumphed for social justices, environmental causes, women's and children's rights and global changes. I believe the circle format is in our blood, passed on from our ancestors and from the very nature of Earth itself. The

Native Americans sat in a circle to listen to one another's opinions because each one has value, each one matters. He or she (and in many tribes it was the female, the Grandmother) takes into consideration all voices and then makes decisions by consensus because it effects the whole group or tribe. Nature teaches us the circle of life through its transformational cycles of seasons and the constant rhythm of life and death. It offers us unlimited teachings and endless opportunities for growth when we are aware of the symbolism. Our souls know all this innately and our minds can be taught to re-member all that we knew long ago.

Returning to Balance

This is the nature of the Divine Feminine or the right brain traits gifted to us: intuition or inner knowing, listening skills, nurturing and caretaking, creativity, dreams and images, thinking with the heart rather than mind, living from a place of spirit rather than dogmas and hierarchal thinking, collaboration and cooperation, being empathetic and compassionate for those less fortunate, caring for our society not from an individual standpoint, but as a Whole. This is the sacred container that we have been blessed with and in which we need to plant seeds and grow, RIGHT NOW.

We must return to the natural state of the human spirit with both the masculine and feminine in balance. In returning to the balance of both, men and women will be able to express themselves freely and be heard with respect and empathy from a place of authenticity and heart. Karen Armstrong, a prominent and prolific author of religious history, states "One of the most urgent tasks of our generation is to build a global community, where men and women of all races, nations and ideologies can live together in peace." I know this community can be built and expanded through the facilitation of intentional healing circles, if available to everyone. Men's groups, such as Mankind Project and Victories for Men, are thankfully offering this work for men, supporting them with programs for a deeper understanding of oneself, better relationships and brighter, more conscious lives.

Circles Benefit All

A Montana retreat brought me full circle into my work. In 2013, I spent a week with Jean Shinoda Bolen, immersed in the theme of her new book *Moving Toward the Millionth Circle*. As I knew she would be, she was inspirational, heart-centered and very funny. She challenged each one of us to take on a new assignment that would be "meaningful, fun and motivated by love". I made the decision shortly after that I would train other women to lead circles and carry on this work. I created a training manual and to date have trained 32 women in the art of facilitating circles. The women are a mix of therapists, social workers, complimentary medicine practitioners, body workers, coaches and leaders in their community.

Bianka is a Licensed Clinical Psychologist and owner of a small group psychotherapy practice in Chicago. She has now led two circles and has been deeply moved by the power of self-exploration in a group of women, both for herself and the other members. Participants leave the group with a sense of deeper connection and purpose, which complements their personal therapy.

Heather, who is a Licensed Massage Therapist and Pain Relief Specialist, took the training and is leading a circle with a different slant. Because of her dance background and understanding of energy, she formed a circle with an experiential focus on the seven Chakra major energy centers and how that knowledge can enhance our body, mind and spirit connection. These are just a couple of examples that illustrate how a circle can be integrated in everyday life for living our visions, opening our hearts and awakening to a greater consciousness.

I have learned so much in circles about women—their dreams and fears, their innate wisdom, their need to nurture and help others before themselves, their deep desire to be accepted and loved. If you had told me in my twenties that I would be doing what I am doing, I would have thought you were crazy. My process of growth and discovery was led by my intuition (listening to my inner voice) and the support of these circles facilitated and taught by many very wise women. Each woman showed up in my life in a synchronistic way, just when I needed them, and sometimes when I didn't know I did! All of my experiences and training have led me to this moment and my heart could not be more open today as a result of these deep experiences.

A Challenge for You

My wish is to inspire and motivate you to go out into the world and take action.

We need to energize the global women's movement with our collective feminine talents and strengths and move forward into a more conscious society. Consciousness means being aware and awake and caring for ALL people, all of nature and the gifts from our Earth. Bringing your awareness and gifts to others will bless and inspire them. You can create the ripples in the pond needed to liberate us from fear and separatism. Each new circle matters!

Act now. Let go of the small voice that says you can't do it! Have the courage to BE the change. I hold you as part of my vision for a better world.

Resources

Suggested Books for the both the leader and participants

The following books are "spiritual classics" that provide inspiration for doing personal work and living an empowered life; they may include readings, insights and questions to use with participants for opening them to greater thinking. They can also assist in finding purpose and passion.

The Invitation, Oriah Mountain Dreamer

I Will Not Die an Unlived Life, Dawna Markova

Circle of Stones, Judith Duerk

I Am a Woman Finding My Own Voice, Janet Quinn

A Year by the Sea and *A Weekend to Change Your Life,* Joan Anderson

A Woman's Book of Life, Joan Borysenko, Ph.D.

The Millionth Circle and *Like a Tree*, Jean Shinoda Bolen

Imagine a Woman in Love with Herself, Patricia Lynn Reilly

These books provide a for deeper understanding of healing and commitment to the process.

A Return to Love, Marianne Williamson

Woman at the Edge of Two Worlds, Lynn Andrews

When Things Fall Apart, and *The Places That Scare You*, Pema Chodron

Excuse Me, Your Life Is Waiting, Lynn Grabhorn

Other inspirational resources

Book of Awakening, Mark Nepo
A beautiful poetic book for daily meditations.

Anatomy of the Spirit, and *Sacred Contracts*, Caroline Myss
Specific teachings on energy medicine and the chakras, with explanations of the patterns we hold, where we hold them in our bodies, and how to heal them.

Wisdom of Menopause, Christiane Northrup
A guide to embracing menopause and creating healing for the changes in your life.

The Dance of the Dissident Daughter, Sue Monk Kidd

The Feminine Face of God, Sherry Ruth Anderson & Patricia Hopkins
Both of the above books describe personal women's journeys into the sacred feminine, and the acceptance of loss or disconnection with particular religions.

The Artist's Way, Julie Cameron
An inspirational guide to living the artist's life, even if you are not an "artist"; can provide for a circle on its own, since it is best done in a group process.

Wherever You Go There You Are, Jon Kabat Zinn
Mindfulness meditation in everyday life, provides great exercises and questions.

Animal Speak and Nature Speak, Ted Andrews
Invaluable resources for nature & animal symbolism.

Mandala, by Judith Cornell, Ph. D
An introductory book on mandala making

Altars, by Denise Linn
Beautifully illustrated ideas about how to create a sacred space.

The Circle of Life: The Heart's Journey Through the Seasons, by Joyce Rupp & Macrina Wiederkehr

Books Suggested Specifically for the Leader

The Millionth Circle, by Jean Shinoda Bolen — A "MUST READ"
How to Change Ourselves and The World through circles. This was
my first inspiration and motivation for starting circles.

Women Who Run with the Wolves, by Clarissa Pinkola Estes, Ph.D.
Myths and Stories of the Wild Woman Archetype; a classic and
profoundly important book for use in understanding archetypal
psychology work. The stories and metaphorical explanations
included could allow for a circle on its own, providing deep
sharing, but each story can also be used for individual themes.

Women's Retreat Book, by Jennifer Louden
A guide to Restoring, Rediscovering, and Reawakening Your True
Self. Includes many useful experiential exercise

Becoming Naturally Therapeutic, by Jacqueline Small
Transpersonal Psychology for Therapists; life-changing guide for
anyone in a therapeutic relationship; includes ten characteristics
that counselors need to discover within themselves, with practical
exercises and sample dialogues.

Books of Prayers

These are good examples of universal or secular prayer.

Illuminata, by Marianne Williamson

Woman Prayers, by Mary Ford-Grabowsky

Earth Prayers and *Live Prayers,* both by Elizabeth Roberts & Elias Amidon

Suggested Music

Karen Drucker

Singer, songwriter, spiritual teacher; music to heal, inspire and empower. There are many CDs and songs with a variety of themes and topics.

Some make great openings or closings to circle. http://www.karendrucker.com/

Helene Van Manen

Earth Chants — Earth Songs

A collection of songs for people who love the Earth and work for peace. Beautiful simple music.
http://www.thevanmanens.com/earthchants.html

David & Steve Gordon

A huge variety of new age and world music, using all types of styles and instruments; all good for background during journaling or artwork.

http://www.sequoiarecords.com/david-and-steve-gordon.html

Libana

Women's vocal group with international sounds, igniting and inspiring the feminine spirit

About the Author

Christine Moses, Founder of Featherheart Holistic Paths, offers counseling and mentoring for body, mind and spirit. Chris creates and facilitates women's circles and retreats for healing and wholeness with heart centered leadership. She believes in the innate wisdom of every individual and is committed to helping others live to their fullest capacity.

She resides in the Chicago area and loves gathering her community for ceremonies and rituals. With her husband, Mike, of thirty-five years, Chris is enjoying her three adult children and is thrilled to have two grandbabies.

Christine offers Women's Circle Facilitation Trainings and other workshops and retreats. Visit her website at
www.chrisfeatherheart.com

Made in the USA
Lexington, KY
20 May 2016